Balanced and Unbalanced Forces

Jenna Winterberg

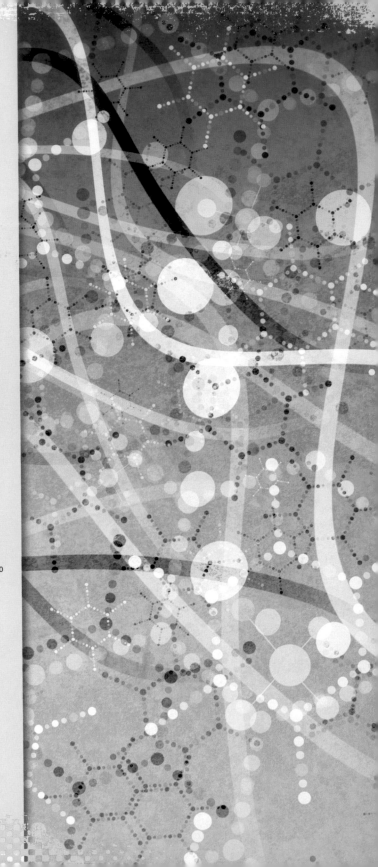

Consultant

Michelle Alfonsi
Engineer, Southern California
Aerospace Industry

Image Credits: Cover & p.1 Gallo Images/Getty
Images; p.7 (bottom) David Burton/Alamy; p.6
North Wind Picture Archives/Alamy; p.22 PCN
Photography/Alamy; pp.4–5 (background) Steven
J. Kazlowski/Alamy; pp.11, 13, 25 (illustrations) Tim
Bradley; pp.6–7 (background), 11 (background), 12
(left), 12 (background), 14–15(background), 18–19
(background), 20–21 (background), 21 (right),
22–23 (background), 24–25 (background), 26
(left), 27, 30–31 (background), 32 iStock; pp.28–29
(illustrations) Janelle Bell-Martin; p.7 (top) TRL Ltd./
Science Source; all other images from Shutterstock.

Library of Congress Cataloging-in-Publication Data

Winterberg, Jenna, author.
  Balanced and unbalanced forces / Jenna Winterberg.
    pages cm
  Summary: "Forces are part of our everyday lives. And
knowing how they work makes us all more powerful!
Balanced forces will keep you upright on your bike.
Unbalanced forces will help you ride your bike as fast as
the wind. Balanced and unbalanced forces play a part in
all that we do."—Provided by publisher.
  Audience: K to grade 3.
  Includes index.
  ISBN 978-1-4807-4646-6 (pbk.)
  ISBN 978-1-4807-5090-6 (ebook)
  1. Force and energy—Juvenile literature.
  2. Energy conversion   Juvenile literature. I. Title.
  QC73.4.W56 2015
  531.6--dc23
                                        2014034270

Teacher Created Materials

5301 Oceanus Drive
Huntington Beach, CA 92649-1030
http://www.tcmpub.com
ISBN 978-1-4807-4646-6

Table of Contents

Let the Battle Begin!

In science, a **force** is any push or pull on an object. Forces get things moving. They stop things, too. They can even change an object's direction. Forces surround us all the time. We can't see or touch them. Usually, we do not even notice them. But they produce powerful effects.

Speed up! Slow down! Push! Pull! Up! Down! Forces are constantly competing with one another. The **magnitude**, number, and direction of forces determine the winner. And the winner determines how objects will move. Game on!

Feel the Force

Try pushing your fingers together. That's a force! There are many types of forces, and some are harder for people to feel than others. But they all have the power to change our world.

Energy and Motion

When a force acts on an object, it transfers energy to that object. The energy causes the object to move, stop, or change direction.

We use three laws to understand how motion works. Sir Isaac Newton came up with these basic rules way back in 1686. The first law says objects keep on doing what they are doing. That means a moving object will keep moving until a force acts on it. For example, a marble will continue to roll until something stops it. The same goes for an object at rest. It won't start moving until a force acts on it. To roll a marble, you need to move it with your hand. Have you ever noticed it's harder to start pedaling your bike than it is to keep it going? That's **inertia** (in-UR-shuh) at work.

Sir Isaac Newton

The Law of Inertia

The first law of motion is the reason we wear seatbelts. Think about what happens when a car brakes suddenly. Your body stays in motion even after the car stops. The belt stops you. If not, your body would continue moving forward at the same speed.

Force Versus Force

Just like 1−1=0, equal forces cancel each other out. When that happens, objects are at rest. If the forces don't cancel each other out (2−1=1), objects move. The direction they move depends on which force is the strongest. And a greater force equals a greater change in movement.

So how do you overcome inertia to get your bike started? You use force. Newton's second law tells us that more force is needed to move a heavier object than a lighter one at the same speed. This law is easier to grasp. We all know pedaling a bike takes energy. And pulling a friend behind your bike takes even more!

What if you get tired of all that pedaling and stop? Newton's third law states that every action has an equal and opposite reaction. That means forces work in pairs. When you sit in a chair, you push down on it. And the chair pushes back up with equal force. The chair does not actively push back. But its solid form stops you from falling through. If the chair pushed back with less force, you would sink into it. With more force, you would shoot up in the air.

Force Versus Inertia

Every force must battle inertia. Inertia is the tendency of an object to resist change to its state of motion. It's the property that tells how much force is needed to stop an object. Or get it moving!

A **vector** measures the magnitude and direction of a force. Scientists use arrows to show vectors. This helps them predict what effect the forces will have on an object. Whatever force is strongest has the biggest effect.

Inertia helps keep you in your seat when you're upside down on a roller coaster.

Contact Forces

Contact forces only act when two objects touch. A few of them are very active in our daily lives.

Friction

Friction occurs when one object moves over another object. This force slows things down. We often see the effects of friction when an object moves across a surface. When you roll a marble on a table, it loses speed. It starts to slow. Then, it stops. Newton's first law tells us a force is acting on it. Otherwise, it would keep moving. The force that stops the marble is friction.

Friction also holds objects in place. Friction prevents sliding. You need friction to keep your shoes tied!

Friction Versus Inertia

A moving soccer ball will travel farther on ice than it will on grass. Grass has more friction. Friction is the force that slows and eventually stops the soccer ball's inertia.

What a Drag!

The amount of friction varies with the objects that are in contact. Wood, glass, and sandpaper all produce different amounts of friction. If you want to slow an object's movement, rough materials, such as grass or sandpaper, will help. If you want to speed up an object, a smooth material, such as glass, works well.

When sandpaper and wood are rubbed together, it creates a lot of friction.

wood

sandpaper

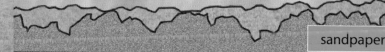

When wood is rubbed against a smoother substance such as glass there is less friction.

wood

glass

Tension

Tension results when an object is pulled in two directions. The object in between, often a string, stretches as a result. This force is the reason we can build bridges. It also holds up arches. And it makes piano music possible.

Applied Force

Applied force transfers from one person or object to another. It's a push. You apply force when you push the buttons on your TV remote. Applied force is what allows us to jump, run, and lift things.

Lift

Lift occurs when an object is in the air and the air is moving. The air pressure above the object becomes lower than the pressure below. Faster air creates a greater lift.

This is the force behind air travel. The high pressure beneath a plane's wings creates lift. Without it, the plane would not be able to fly.

The more tension there is on guitar strings, the higher the pitch will be.

Tension Versus Gravity

When an object starts to move, it can take a while for the motion to travel through the entire object. Get a friend to record a movie of this experiment. Then, play it back slowly. This happens fast!

TENSION

GRAVITY

Loosely dangle a Slinky about a foot off the ground. Note: The Slinky is at rest because it's being pulled up just as hard as it's being pulled down by **gravity**.

Let the Slinky go, and watch the bottom. If you missed it, watch your video in slow motion. You should see the top of the Slinky start to fall before the bottom. But the bottom floats mysteriously in the air!

Why didn't gravity pull the bottom of the Slinky down with the top? Because the tension pulling up on the Slinky is equal to the pull of gravity.

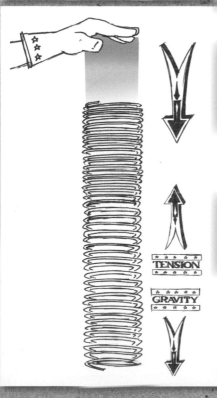

TENSION

GRAVITY

The crazy thing is that when anything falls, it falls like a Slinky. Whether it's a pen or a porcupine, the top starts falling before the bottom does.

Normal Force

Normal force is present when two objects rest on each other. Normal force supports the pillows on a bed. Think back to the example of the chair from earlier. Your body pushes down on your chair. The chair pushes back to hold you up. Your solid chair uses normal force to support you. It's doing it right now!

Air Resistance

Like friction, **air resistance** slows objects. Sometimes air resistance is referred to as *drag*. The force is greater when objects travel at high speeds. It is also greater when objects have a larger surface.

Engineers reduce air resistance by making cars and airplanes with smooth surfaces and streamlined shapes. But some people depend on air resistance to fuel their fun, such as windsurfers and skydivers.

normal force

gravity

Lift Versus Air Resistance

When an airplane attempts to defy gravity, lift and **thrust** help make it happen.

Air resistance drags the airplane backward.

Lift pushes the airplane up.

Gravity pulls the airplane down.

With the help of a motor, thrust overcomes air resistance and gravity.

Distant Forces

Not all forces need to touch objects to act on them. Distant forces act without contact. Three major forces make up this group.

Gravity

Gravity is a force that acts between objects, pulling one toward the other. Earth's gravity acts on any object that has mass. Mass is the amount of **matter** in an object. Weight measures gravity's pull. Planets with more mass than Earth have more gravity. Jupiter's mass is 300 times greater than Earth's. So you would weigh 300 times more on Jupiter than you do on Earth.

Gravity is always present, so we don't take much note of it. But it's the reason we can stand. And sit. And walk! It pulls us to the ground. Without it, we would float, as if we were in space.

Watch Out!

Objects with more mass respond more slowly to force because their mass increases their inertia. That makes it harder to move more massive objects. But it also makes them harder to stop!

Electric Force

Electric force occurs between two objects with a charge. Objects can have a positive or negative charge. Opposite charges attract. But two objects with the same charge will push each other away.

This force starts with tiny **atoms**. Every atom is made up of even smaller parts. One of those is the electron. Electrons have a negative charge. They orbit the nucleus, or center, of an atom. The nucleus holds neutrons. Neutrons have no charge. They are neutral. The nucleus also holds protons. Protons are positive. Positive protons attract negative electrons. As a result, electrons stay in orbit. That's the electric force.

Electric force also causes electrons to leave atoms. Electrons are attracted to atoms with more protons than electrons. Those atoms have a greater positive charge. Electrons can jump from one atom to the next. This electric force makes **electricity**. Electricity provides us with light in our homes and schools. It also allows us to talk on cell phones and watch TV. They're tiny, but atoms can make a big difference!

Electric Force Versus Gravity

Gravity pulls large objects, like the moon, into orbit with Earth. But when it comes to the tiny atoms that make up our entire universe, it's actually electrical force that cause electrons to circle protons.

protons and neutrons

electron

Electric force is like an invisible spring— as the charges move farther apart, a weaker spring pulls them together.

Magnetic Force

Magnetic force attracts metals like iron and steel. But it doesn't work on most other metals. It also doesn't work on nonmetals. Magnetic force has no pull on glass, plastic, or wood.

Every magnet has two poles: north and south. Both poles attract metal equally. And the opposite poles of two magnets will pull each other close. But this force can do more than just attract. Magnetic force can also repel, or push apart. The same poles of two magnets will repel each other.

Earth is also a magnet. A giant one! We use its force to navigate, or find our way to places. A compass needle always points toward the north pole of the Earth's magnet. It's not the same as the North Pole, but they are near each other. This information helps people figure out where they are and where they need to be.

Electric force and magnetic force combine
to create electromagnetic force.

Magnetic Force Versus Gravity

In a match between gravity and the other forces, gravity usually loses. You can see just how weak gravity is by using a magnet to pick up a pile of paper clips. No question, magnetic force wins!

Combined Forces

It's rare for a force to act alone. Think about Newton's laws again. The third law describes forces acting in pairs—for every action, there is an equal and opposite reaction. Even when you stand still, more than one force is acting on you. Earth pulls you down with the force of gravity. But the ground also pushes you up using normal force.

When forces act and react with equal force, they create **balance**. Balanced forces can keep objects still. They can also keep objects moving. Think back to the bicycle that uses Newton's laws. Friction, air resistance, and gravity all combine to make it possible to ride your bike.

Combining Vectors

Vectors help scientists see how forces might combine to affect an object. These arrows show what happens if applied force acts on an object from two different directions.

Engineers put a lot of time and energy into balancing forces. What would happen if they didn't? Planes wouldn't fly. Dams wouldn't hold. Buildings wouldn't stand.

When forces acting on an object are not equal in strength, they are unbalanced. Unbalanced forces always result in a change in movement. The change can be in direction, speed, or both. Change isn't always a bad thing. Think about Newton's first law. Objects in motion stay in motion. Objects at rest stay at rest. Unbalanced forces are necessary to change that.

Unbalanced forces make driving possible. We speed up, slow down, and steer because of them. They also set sports in motion. They let us kick a ball forward and throw it in the air. They even help engineers destroy old buildings so new ones can be built!

The Engineering Process

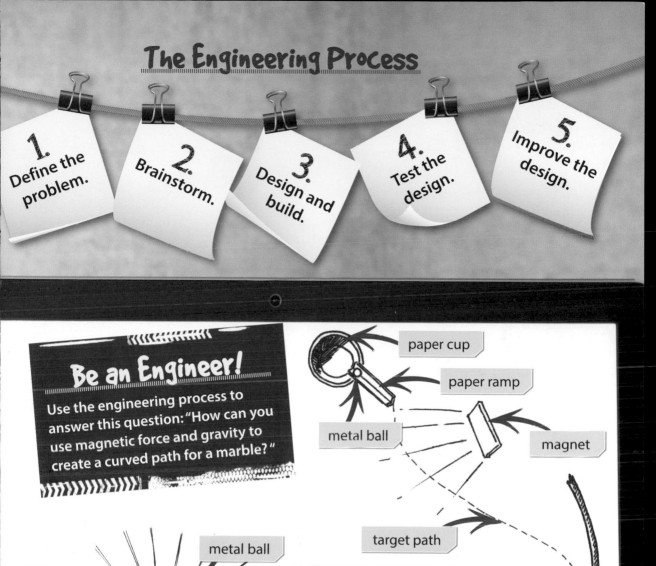

Be an Engineer!

Use the engineering process to answer this question: "How can you use magnetic force and gravity to create a curved path for a marble?"

paper cup

paper ramp

metal ball

magnet

target path

metal ball

paper cup

gravity

Test your ideas by rolling the ball down the paper ramp. Does it follow the target path? If not, move the pieces around to intensify the effects.

paper ramp

rope to catch stray balls

And the Winner Is...

Any time there is a change in direction or speed, a force is present. And these forces are powerful. Whether it's gravity pulling down or a jolt from an electric charge, forces get things moving!

Understanding all these forces is challenging. But living without them would be even more difficult. Without them, we wouldn't have electricity. There would be no TV. There would be no cars to drive. We couldn't walk. There wouldn't even be anywhere to walk.

Everyone relies on forces. Engineers study forces to build everything from forks to massive houses. Athletes use forces to help them score goals. Even musicians use forces to produce music. It looks like in the battle of the forces, the real winner is us!

Think Like a Scientist

What happens when lift, gravity, and air resistance act on an object? Experiment and find out!

What to Get

- ⊃ golf ball
- ⊃ hair dryer
- ⊃ table tennis balls

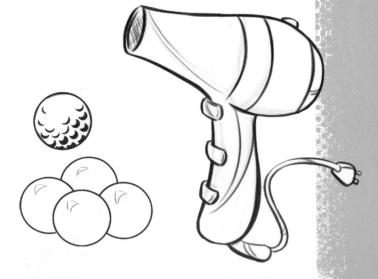

What to Do

1 Plug in the hair dryer, and turn it on. Place it on the highest setting and point it straight up in the air.

2 Before you place a table tennis ball above the air stream, write what you expect to see. Now, place the ball over the blowing air. Observe the results.

3 Try adding more balls slowly, and record your results. Try using a golf ball, too.

4 How many balls will float at once? What would happen if you turned the hair dryer to low? Is this an example of balanced or unbalanced forces? Which forces are involved?

Ball	Prediction	Result
table tennis		
golf		

Glossary

air resistance—the drag on something caused by moving though air

atoms—tiny particles that make up all matter

balance—a state in which different things are equal

electricity—a form of energy made up of a stream of electrons

force—a push or pull on an object

friction—the force that causes a moving object to slow down when it is touching another object

gravity—a force that acts between objects, pulling one toward the other

inertia—property of matter in which still objects stay at rest and moving objects keep moving at the same speed in the same direction

magnetic—having the power to attract certain metals

magnitude—the size or power of something

matter—anything that has mass and takes up space

thrust—a forward or upward push

vector—a quantity that has size and direction

Index

Your Turn!

Furry Force

Watch your pet or a friend's pet as it plays and rests. What forces act on the animal? What forces are balanced? Unbalanced? Keep a log of what you observe.